WEEKLY WR READER
EARLY LEARNING LIBRARY

Where People **Work**
¿Dónde **trabaja** la gente?

What Happens at a
Toy Factory?

¿Qué pasa en
una fábrica de juguetes?

by/por Kathleen Pohl

Reading consultant/Consultora de lectura: Susan Nations, M.Ed., author, literacy coach,
consultant in literacy development/autora, tutora de alfabetización, consultora de desarrollo de la lectura

Please visit our web site at: www.garethstevens.com
For a free color catalog describing Weekly Reader® Early Learning Library's list
of high-quality books, call 1-877-445-5824 (USA) or 1-800-387-3178 (Canada).
Weekly Reader® Early Learning Library's fax: (414) 336-0164.

Library of Congress Cataloging-in-Publication Data

Pohl, Kathleen.
  What happens at a toy factory? = ¿Qué pasa en una fábrica de juguetes? / Kathleen Pohl.
    p. cm. — (Where people work = ¿Dónde trabaja la gente?)
  Includes bibliographical references and index.
  ISBN-10: 0-8368-7390-4 — ISBN-13: 978-0-8368-7390-0 (lib. bdg.)
  ISBN-10: 0-8368-7397-1 — ISBN-13: 978-0-8368-7397-9 (softcover)
    1. Toys—Design and construction—Juvenile literature. I. Title.
  II. Title: ¿Qué pasa en una fábrica de juguetes?
  TS2301.T7P5418   2007
  688.7'2—dc22   2006016876

This edition first published in 2007 by
Weekly Reader® Early Learning Library
A Member of the WRC Media Family of Companies
330 West Olive Street, Suite 100
Milwaukee, Wisconsin 53212 USA

Buddy® is a registered trademark of Weekly Reader Corporation. Used under license.

Managing editor: Dorothy L. Gibbs
Art direction: Tammy West
Cover design and page layout: Scott M. Krall
Photo research: Diane Laska-Swanke
Translation: Tatiana Acosta and Guillermo Gutiérrez

Photographs copyright © K'NEX Industries, Inc., 2006. Reprinted with permission.

Acknowledgement: The publisher thanks K'NEX Industries, Inc. and Stewart and Diana McMeeking
for their expert consulting, the use of their facilities, and their kind assistance in developing this book.

Printed in the United States of America

1 2 3 4 5 6 7 8 9 10 09 08 07 06

Hi, Kids!

I'm Buddy, your Weekly Reader® pal. Have you ever visited a toy factory? I'm here to show and tell what happens inside a toy factory. So, come on. Turn the page and read along!

– – – – – – – –

¡Hola, chicos!

Soy Buddy, su amigo de Weekly Reader®.
¿Han estado alguna vez en una fábrica de juguetes? Estoy aquí para contarles lo que pasa en una fábrica de juguetes. Así que vengan conmigo. ¡Pasen la página y vamos a leer!

Look at all these toys! They are toys you can build yourself. This toy **factory** makes building sets.

– – – – – – – –

¡Miren todos estos juguetes! Son juguetes que se pueden armar. Esta **fábrica** de juguetes hace juegos de construcción.

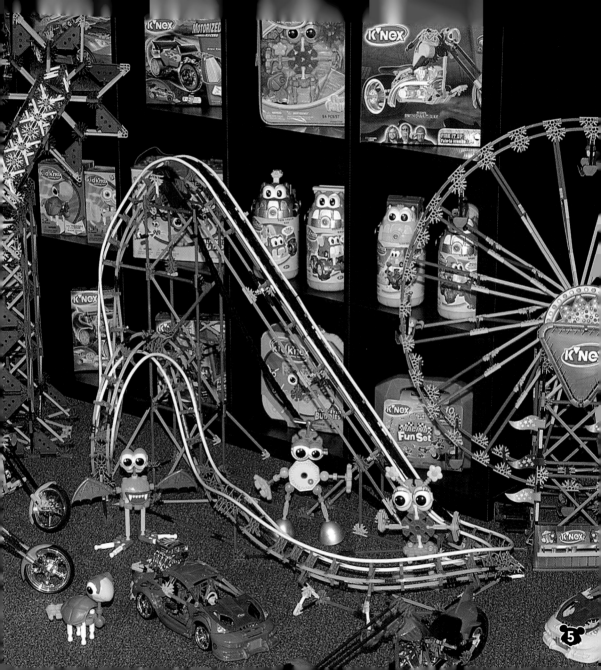

First, workers think of a fun toy to build. Pictures give them good ideas. Next, a worker draws the toy on paper.

— — — — — — — —

Primero, los trabajadores piensan en un juguete que pueda ser divertido. Miran fotografías para tener buenas ideas. Después, un trabajador dibuja el juguete en papel.

Another worker makes a **model** of the toy. The model shows the toy's size and shape.

- - - - - - - - -

Otro trabajador hace un **modelo** del juguete. El modelo muestra el tamaño y la forma del juguete.

model/modelo

A building set has many plastic pieces. A **steel mold**, or form, shapes each piece. Molds are made in a place called a **tooling shop**.

– – – – – – – – –

Un juego de construcción tiene muchas piezas de plástico. Cada pieza se forma en un **molde de acero**. Los moldes se hacen en un lugar llamado **taller de fabricación**.

steel mold/
molde de acero

plastic pieces/
piezas de plástico

11

This worker is making a piece for a building set. He puts a mold into a special machine. A steel mold is very heavy!

— — — — — — — — —

Este trabajador está haciendo una pieza de un juego de construcción. Pone un molde dentro de una máquina especial. ¡Un molde de acero es muy pesado!

steel mold/
molde de acero

Tiny bits of plastic go into the machine, too. Heat melts the plastic in the mold. The plastic shapes cool and harden. Then the machine spits them out.

— — — — — — — — —

Dentro de la máquina se meten también pequeños trozos de plástico. El calor funde el plástico en el molde. Las piezas de plástico se enfrían y endurecen. Después, la máquina las escupe.

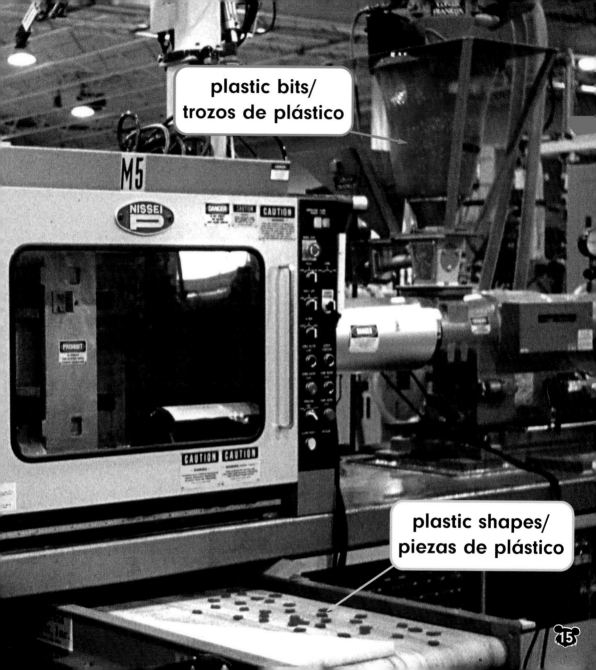

plastic bits/
trozos de plástico

plastic shapes/
piezas de plástico

15

Each building set needs directions. A worker makes them up on a computer. The directions tell how to build the toy.

— — — — — — — —

Cada juego de construcción necesita unas instrucciones. Un trabajador las hace en una computadora. Las instrucciones explican cómo armar el juego.

Kids come to test the building set. They follow the directions to build the toy. They help make sure the building set works.

– – – – – – – –

Algunos niños vienen a probar el juego. Siguen las instrucciones para armarlo. Ayudan a comprobar que el juego funciona bien.

Each building set comes packed in a box. Wow! Look at this set! It is ready to take home and build.

– – – – – – – – –

Cada juego de construcción viene empacado en una caja. ¡Caramba! ¡Mira este juego! Ya está listo para que alguien se lo lleve a casa y se ponga a construir.

 # Glossary/Glosario

directions — words and pictures that tell how to do something or make something

factory — a place where many machines and workers make things

model — a sample of a new toy or some other object that shows what it will look like

mold — a hollow form that keeps hot liquid in a certain shape until it cools and becomes hard

steel — a hard, strong metal made of iron

tooling shop — a place where workers make steel molds and other parts for machines

— — — — — — — —

acero — metal duro y fuerte que se hace con hierro

fábrica — lugar donde muchos trabajadores hacen algo usando máquinas

instrucciones — palabras e imágenes que explican cómo hacer algo

modelo — muestra de un juguete nuevo o de cualquier otro objeto que permite ver cómo será

molde — recipiente hueco donde se pone un líquido caliente para que se enfríe y tome su forma

taller de fabricación — lugar donde los trabajadores hacen moldes de acero y otras partes de máquinas

 # For More Information/Más información

Books/Libros

From Idea to Toy. Start to Finish (series). Ali Mitgutsch
  (Carolrhoda Books)

La fábrica de camiones de bomberos. Lee y aprende (series).
  Catherine Anderson (Heinemann Library)

Let's Visit a Toy Factory. Miriam Anne Bourne
  (Troll Communications)

Teddy Bears from Start to Finish. Made in the USA (series).
  Tanya Lee Stone (Blackbirch Press)

Index/Índice

About the Author

Kathleen Pohl has written and edited many children's books. Among them are animal tales, rhyming books, retold classics, and the forty-book series *Nature Close-Ups*. She also served for many years as top editor of *Taste of Home* and *Country Woman* magazines. She and her husband, Bruce, live among beautiful Wisconsin woods and share their home with six goats, a llama, and all kinds of wonderful woodland creatures.

Información sobre la autora

Kathleen Pohl ha escrito y corregido muchos libros infantiles. Entre ellos hay cuentos de animales, libros de rimas, versiones nuevas de cuentos clásicos y la serie de cuarenta libros *Nature Close-Ups*. Además, trabajó durante muchos años como directora de las revistas *Taste of Home* y *Country Woman*. Kathleen vive con su marido, Bruce, en los bellos bosques de Wisconsin. Ambos comparten su hogar con seis cabras, una llama y todo tipo de maravillosos animales del bosque.